For the letters, the profile, and some of the
memorials, the collector is indebted to Mr. Allen,
of Liskeard. The shadow is from Mrs. M.
Welsford, in whose family, (also claiming rela-
tionship by marriage) it has been carefully
treasured.

Table of Contents.

MEMORIALS, &c.

WILLIAM COOKWORTHY, was born at Kingsbridge, in 1705. His mother was left a widow, with I think five sons—William, Philip, Benjamin, Joseph, and Jacob, and some daughters. Whether before or after she lost her husband I do not know, but nearly all their property was sunk in the South Sea Stock Speculation; so that she was greatly reduced in circumstances, and obliged to send her sons out into the world early in life. William and Jacob went into the drug business, at Plymouth, about the same time. Their mother retired to a small house at Kingsbridge, opposite the entrance to Duncombe Street; and maintained herself and daughters in great respectability by dressmaking, and took apprentices to that business. She was obliged to live in a very humble, economical manner, sometimes allowing only one pound of pork for dinner for the family.

At length things began to mend; the sons William and Jacob got forward in the drug business; and the Mother went to live with them in Nut Street, Plymouth; and was allowed by them to be a liberal benefactor to the poor, which afforded her great pleasure.

From his great-niece at Kingsbridge.

The earlier part of his life, though within the bounds of morality, was spent in an apparent distance from the principles of our profession, in which he was educated; yet his judgment seemed to have been early convinced of their propriety and consistency with the Scriptures, as he was often, in this period, called upon in various companies to defend them.

Towards the 31st year of his age, the power of truth took more effectual hold of his mind; and gradually submitting, in the course of some years, to its operation; he at length thought it necessary to retire from his outward affairs, that the dispensation he was under might accomplish the great end for which it was administered. In this retirement, a blessed and happy change was wrought, by a submission of his own to the divine will; and laying aside his acquired knowledge, and all dependence on the natural abilities of unenlightened reason, he followed his good guide on the way to the cross, and accepted with ready obedience a gift in the ministry.

Intent upon improving the talent committed to his trust, he laboured diligently in the western counties, and also in places more distant when he apprehended himself called thereto. For about 25 years he held a meeting at his own house, every first day evening when at home, and permitted by health; at first designed for his own family, but it was soon attended by most of the younger friends in this place, and frequently to their great satisfaction. In the exercise of his gift, he was mostly concerned to address his auditory in the pathetic persuasive language of love, whether it was to encourage, to exhort, or even to reprove or reclaim. To the poor, the afflicted, and the mourner, he was remarkably a true son of consolation, by the healing balm through him administered to their several states. In the discipline of the Church, he was concerned to reclaim offenders, by repeated attempts to convince them of the impropriety and consequences of inconsistent or disorderly conduct; not to draw over them the line of severity, except where lenity was inadmissible—but in all cases the tenderness and love which so eminently marked the performance of his religious and social duties, were never suspended. Sound in judgment, and of a most comprehensive mind, humane and benevolent in the highest degree, attached to no party, open to conviction, (though steady in his religious principles) his chief views were directed to the general good of mankind, so that he may be said to have fulfilled that excellent precept " to do good and to communicate, forget not." In the course of his business, as well as on account of his extensive knowledge, he was often in company with men eminent for their abilities or superior rank ; and as we believe that on such occasions his conversation and address were consistent with his religious profession, he thereby exhibited a sterling example of the superiority of Christian simplicity, over the vanity and absurdities of the manners and customs of the world.

So far Testimony of Monthly Meeting,
Plymouth, 4th 3rd Month, 1781.

His eloquence in conversation was not (like that of Coleridge) an unintermitting flow of overwhelming oratory : he practised the principle of give and take, and would stop to answer the question of a child, if asked in the spirit of improvement. But it sometimes betrayed him into singular unobservance of circumstances ; as taking his neighbour's glass when he had emptied his own ; and breaking one of a beautiful set of china, to shew the owner the excellence of the texture. And this intensity of thought was accompanied by rare powers of abstraction. Walking in full conversation up to the door of his place of worship ; he no sooner entered, than every thought of this world was suppressed, and his whole mind concentrated upon the sacred purpose of the meeting.

In 1745 an American brought him specimens of CHINA CLAY, (Kaolin) and CHINA STONE, (Petunze) found in Virginia ; and of Porcelain, made therefrom. (See Letter A.)

At this time much curiosity existed, on this subject, by Count Reaumur's report, in 1729, on the materials of the Chinese porcelain, sent home by father D'Entrecolles ; which had originated the manufacture of Sevres ; and by the accidental discovery of the like process at Dresden.

This hint from the American, may have set him on the investigation : for we find in

Polwhele's History of Cornwall ;

Among the burrows of a mine near Helstone, the late ingenious Mr. Cookworthy discovered a sort of earth which partly gave occasion to his porcelain manufactory at Plymouth.

The substance had the distinguishing characters of the Kaolin of China ; which is described to be a white, unctuous, unvitrifiable earth ; and is considered by the Chinese as the bones of Chinaware, or what gives it its firmness and consistency in the fire. The Petunze, or vitrifiable ingredient (says Mr. Cookworthy) which the Chinese consider as the flesh, since it gives the body transparency, softness of texture, and lustre in the breaking, was yet to be discovered. In his search after this, Mr. C. found a stone which would vitrify ; but after some pretty extensive experiments, was satisfied it would not answer. This was a compound stone having a small mixture of limestone particles in it.

Some time after this he perceived that our western granite or Moorstone was of the genus of the stone he was enquiring after ; as it was sufficiently vitrifiable.

On giving a piece of this stone a white heat, in a crucible,
it melted; and the white parts of the Stone were of a beautiful, glassy, semi-diaphanous white; but the black particles
burning red, as containing iron, and being by any practicable
art inseparable from the white part; it was plain the common
moorstone would not answer, in so elegant a ware as the
porcelain; where the perfection of the white is its merit and
excellence.   At length he discovered what he wanted near
St. Austell.

So far Polwhele.

Of this discovery we are told by *Mr. R. Martin, of the
St. Austell Blowing House, (date 19th October, 1853.)* That
he lodged in Carlogges, at St. Stephen's parish, with Mr.
Richard Yelland, the Grandfather of my informant, who is
himself about 70 years of age; and during that time made the
discovery; he has heard that he used to go about the Country
searching for minerals, and used to employ the ' Dowsing Rod.'
(See page 7.) It is reported that he first discovered it in St.
Columb Church, or rather in the Tower, which is built of stone
from St. Stephen's.   After having been worked for some time,
it would appear to have been almost abandoned; as about
sixty years ago, Mr. Yelland informed me, that he, when a
little boy, was engaged with his Father and three or four
others, in raising China-Clay, and that the quantity then
produced, about 100 tons a year, (See page 7) was considered
to be more than the markets would bear.

The precise date of this first discovery is not given, but we
find in *Borlase*, that " in 1758, Mr. Cookworthy of Plymouth,
had made experiments on the Breage chinastone, and that it
had been found useful in the making of Porcelain:" hence it
was probably some years before that; not far from 1755.   Nor
have we any further distinct accounts of it till the establish-
ment of the patent.

Lord Camelford writes to Polwhele :—

" Boconnoc, Nov. 30, 1790.
" Dear Sir,   •

" With regard to the Porcelain Manufactory,
that was attemped to be established some years ago, and which
was afterwards transferred to Bristol, where it failed; it was
undertaken by Mr. Cookworthy, upon a *friend of his* having
discovered on an estate of mine in the parish of St. Stephen's,
a certain white saponaceous clay; and close by it, a species of

granite or moorstone, white with greenish spots; which he immediately perceived to be the two materials described by the Missionary Pére D'Entrecolles, as the constituent parts of the Chinese porcelain; the one giving whiteness and body to the paste, the other vitrification and transparency. The difficulties found in proportioning properly these materials, so as to give exactly the necessary degree of vitrification, and no more, and other niceties with regard to the manipulation, discouraged us from proceeding in this concern; after we had procured a patent for the use of our materials, and expended on it between two and three thousand pounds. We then sold our interest to Mr. Champion, of Bristol."

So far Lord Camelford.

From the words "we" and "us," Lord Camelford appears to have been his partner.

The works were established at Coxside, where the buildings, &c. still continue as a Shipwright's yard and offices. And many specimens remain, exemplifying the gradual progress of the work, from fire cracks, warping, bad colour, glaze in blotches from imperfect fusion, and painting run and tarnished; up to the purest white in body and glaze, the most delicate and exquisite painting, and the enamelling, and projecting shells, leaves, and flowers, free from distortion on their thinest edges. But details of this progress *in the works*, even traditionary, the compiler has been quite unable to obtain.

They are said to have procured an excellent painter and enameller from Sevres; and Bone, the distinguished British enameller is known to have served his apprenticeship there.*

The next account we have, is from the *History of the Staffordshire Potteries, Hanley*, 1827, collected, in great part, from the personal recollections of then aged potters. From this we learn :—

Mr. Cookworthy having discovered in what are now called the Cornish Clay and Growan Stone, similar materials to the Kaolin and Petunze, he first attempted the manufacture of porcelain, and being tolerably successful, he obtained a patent in 1768 for the exclusive use of these materials in the manufacture of Porcelain and Pottery. He afterwards sold the patent right to R. Champion, Esq. a respectable merchant in Bristol, who

---

* In Burt's "Review, &c. of Plymouth," 1816, (page 174); it is said on the authority of one " employed on the China Works in his youthful days," that there was such a demand for their enamelled blue and white china, both at home and in America, both ornamental and useful, that they could hardly be made fast enough. That from 50 to 60 persons were engaged in its various processes; and that the fuel consumed was chiefly wood.

had been long employed in investigating the properties of porcelain. He erected a manufactory in that city, in which for some time he pursued his experiments, and ultimately succeeded in bringing to a state of perfection, rivalling the Oriental productions; and although this is the first real English porcelain, (for it has the essential property, being indestructible in both body and glaze), yet he expended a large fortune in erecting the various requisite premises; and after fully completing his scheme, was so unsuccessful in obtaining a demand adequate to the expenditure, that about 1777 he sold the patent to a company in Staffordshire.

Mr. Cookworthy was doubtless a person of considerable ability; but according to the information concerning him, from relations and Mr. Champion, he was constantly so very eager in acquiring knowledge, that he seldom could find leisure to communicate to others his own stores of information. Hence all there is to commemorate him, are a few letters and essays* in the periodicals of that day, and this discovery of materials for making porcelain. Indeed this last will immortalise him, for it is the general conviction of potters (1827), that the greatest service ever conferred by one person on the pottery manufacture, is that of his making them acquainted with the nature and properties of the materials, and his introduction of Growan Stone for either body or glaze, or both when requisite. Without it we should want our fine porcelain so deservedly admired; neither should we have the excellent cream colour and elegant blue painted now in constant demand. For when Mr. Champion petitioned Parliament for an act, authorising the extension of his patent for a further period of fourteen years, the manufacturers of cream colour or Queen's ware, among whom was Mr. J. Wedgewood and Mr. Turner, (*and who had never made any porcelain*) brought forward as an objection to its extension, the restriction of all others from employing Cornish stone in the *other* branches of the manufacture, in which it would be of great advantage. They therefore opposed the bill, and (with the aid of Earl Gower), obtained an alteration, which, while it confirmed to Mr. Champion the sole and exclusive application of the Cornish clay and stone, for the manufacture of *transparent* ware, however it might be named, porcelain or any other designation; it allowed the potters generally the free use of the stone, in the *opacous* glazes, and of the clay in *opaque*

---

* None of these, (except that on the Divining Rod); has J. P. been able to find: not even the treatise on furnaces mentioned in his letter (A).

pottery, by which that ware was greatly improved in solidity, durability, and texture; and rendered greatly superior to any before manufactured.

(From the same authority we also learn, that he first instituted in this country, the manufacture of Cobalt blue, direct from the ore. *As follows.)*

In the early process of *blue painting*, the colour was prepared by grinding foreign imported zaffres with muller and slab. But the demand increasing, we are informed that William Cookworthy, who had been a painter, (of porcelain) and also a chemist and druggist; at Bristol happening to meet an old acquaintance, Roger Kenniston, also a painter, in very reduced circumstances; fully instructed him in the process of making a blue from zaffre, and also the whole recipe for extracting the pure metal from Cobalt ores.

So far the History of Staffordshire Potteries.

The progress of this art, in Stafford and Worcester shires, to the rank of one of the great manufactures of the country; and its competition with the finest works of Sevres and Dresden at the Great Exhibition, are known to all. But it is fair to our honoured townsman to say, that intrinsic excellence has been largely sacrificed to appearance and cheapness. Little if any, of the modern British China, is equal in texture, to the latest old Plymouth and Bristol specimens now remaining.

The manufacture has followed the fuel; but the clay and stone are still with us, and their joint products amounted last year to upwards of 100,000 tons, returning something like £150,000 a year to the industry of the adjoining counties— the benefits of his discovery, now seventy years after his decease. (See back, page 4.)

In his regular business of a chemist, he also improved several of the medicinal preparations of his day.

The enthusiasm of his character did not stop at practical and intelligible science. He is said to have been a full believer in the Divining or Dowsing rod, for discovering metallic veins by occult magnetic attraction. (See back, page 4.) A pretty long treatise on its virtues, with minute instructions for its use is given on his authority in Price's Treatise on Mining;

drawn mostly it would appear from Agricola and others, but without any expression of doubt or question on his part. And he was, in common with many learned men of his day, a disciple of Swedenborg; (Letter E.) apparently before he was personally acquainted with him, or the knowledge of Swedenborg's high scientific attainments had given them a common interest of a more tangible kind. (See Preface.)

However fanciful these notions may have been, and still be, considered, may we not ask, without professing conviction to either of them, whether the magnetic odyle of Reichenbach, and the curious cases of mesmeric clearsight, do not now give them respectively, at least more analogical probability than they ever possessed before?

He was duly esteemed by the scientific men of his day; his grandson keeps as a relic, the table, round which Capt. Cook, Sir Jos. Banks, and Dr. Solander dined with him, just before their famous voyage round the world; and the concourse at his funeral (page 9) was by no means limited to inhabitants of the neigbourhood. The estimation in which he was held by his fellow townsmen may be perceived by the following memorial.

To the memory of W. Cookworthy, late of Plymouth, a Minister amongst the people called Quakers, and an eminent Chemist, who died the 16th of 10th Mo. 1780, aged 76.

The pious character of this great and good man is so generally known, that it is not possible to be buried in oblivion, yet every Christian mind will be desirous of preserving memorials of persons eminent in religion.

As a Minister, he was clear, pathetic, engaging, persuasive beyond all language and indefatigably assiduous.

As a Parent, he was sacredly watchful in his examples, affectionately tender in his advice, and a constant encourager of piety and virtue.

As a Member of Society, he was a promoter and preserver of harmony, peace, and good will, and few have more essentially contributed to its real happiness.

As a Friend, through Christian tenderness and true sympathy, his mind was ever susceptible of the finest feelings of humanity. To the poor benevolently kind; to the rich a pattern of condescension; and to all, an engaging and desirable companion. As a man and Christian, he shone in literature, more so in science, and most of all in religion. Through Christian meekness, conscious innocence and integrity, he bore unmerited censure with the greatest contentment. Steady and indefatigable in the prosecution of laudable and religious designs, he seldom failed of success. In short, his profound depth of understanding, his great knowledge in literature, practise in science, and experience in religion, rendered his company pleasing and instructive to every class of people, and was most esteemed where he was most known. While he shone as the scholar, philosopher, and Christian, he exampled us in the most child-like simplicity, and dependence upon the great Universal Parent.

He was comely in person, kind and charitable in his disposition: courteous and truly polite in his carriage beyond all forms of breeding, he united the ease and affability of the true gentleman, with the sobriety and dignity of the sincere Christian.

Thus far the Memorial.

When the French fleet appeared off, in 1779, he of course, as a Quaker, could not fight; but he seems to have recommended, though 75 years of age, that the Quakers should have charge of the women and children, and convey them to a place of safety, in case of the expected attack.

In the following year 1780, he was withdrawn from the wide circle, to which he was a revered and loved example: and of the interesting bedside notes of his relatives, during his illness, it will be enough here to quote the closing scene.

" His speech is now so much altered that it is hardly intelligible."

" He sometimes looks up, with such a sweet smile on his countenance as no words can express. It is a heavenly appearance; far surpassing anything I ever saw in his health. He is quite sensible, and says he shall go without sigh or groan."

" He died this morning, soon after seven o'clock; without a struggle. I was at the bedside at the time, but could not distinguish the instant he quitted mortality."

The attendance at his funeral exhibited, in coincidence with the memoir at page 8, the high esteem in which he was held.

" Last 1st day, the remains of our dear friend were removed from his house about two in the afternoon; the number of people who attended at the door, with the large addition made as the corpse passed along, was very great—hundreds more than the meeting-house would contain—so that we had much difficulty to get in. After some little time the people were very still."

MEMORIALS, ETC.

Such are the scanty records of one, who was the honour of Plymouth 100 years ago; yet whose name does not appear on our Local Chronologies, nor in any Biographical Dictionary, to which the writer has had access. If the present century should bring us another like him, let us hope that he will be better remembered.

NOTE to p. 4.

The expression in Lord Camelford's letter "*a friend of his*," (italics by J. P.) seems to have been a misapprehension of the American discovery, mentioned in letter (A). All the accounts, written and traditionary, attribute the discovery, in Cornwall, to W. Cookworthy ; who was not one to accept the reputation due to another.

His remaining letters being chiefly religious, it seemed desirable to print only enough of them to let the reader into the habitual state of his thoughts and feelings: this not being intended as a book of instruction, further than by example.

LETTERS.

A.—*Objection to Prize Goods—China Clay in America—Chemical Writings and Discoveries.*

To *Richard Hingston.*

Plymouth, 30th of 5th Month, 1745.

Dear Richard,

My Eastern and South Ham journies have kept me of late so much abroad, that I have not had opportunities of writing to thee, equal to my inclination.

Thy last order went a few days since, by W. John's barge, for Falmouth; which is the first opportunity that has offered since we received it. Amos has I understand answered thy question about the beds, &c. I hope his reply is fully satisfactory.

We have, of late, been very barren in news; but a few days since, we had certain advice, that Admiral Martin's squadron, had taken a very rich ship from the Havannah; though the Captain, from whom Char de Voigne has received a letter, says she came from St. Domingo. It is allowed, however, that she has a good deal of money on board; and so it is likely she may have been at both places. Char de Voigne tells me, that Cape Breton is of such consequence to the French, that they cannot do without it; and we may depend on their exerting their utmost endeavours to retake it; and if they should not be successful, would never make peace without its reddition.

We had a very considerable sale here, for the cargoes of the prizes taken by Martin's Squadron, some time since; and that of the Elephant. J. Colesworthy was at it; and bought a very large quantity of sugar on commission; as well as another friend from London, whose name is Jonathan Gurnell. We must not be at all surprised at this; it being, by what I can find, grown a settled maxim, that friends may deal in prize goods. For on my attacking F. Jewel, for being concerned in the purchase of the Mentor, which he bought in partnership with Dr. Duker, and Lancelot Robinson; he pleaded, in his justification, that friends at London were clearly of opinion, there is no harm in it; and that John Hayward, a preacher, had given him a commission, to buy prize Havanah Snuffs; and brother F. who has done something in this way too, acquaints me, that friend Willson, when here, seemed to be quite ignorant of anything wrong in the practice, and only advised, in general, that friends should not act against their conviction. I am not at present disposed to make reflections; and therefore shall only say, that I hope I shall be kept clear of it; as I believe it would bring a cloud over my mind.

I purpose, next second day, to set out for the West; and hope to be with thee about the 22nd proximo: but I shall not be able to stay, as usual; as I must hasten to Looe, to 'squire Sally to Redruth yearly meeting; from whence she proposes to go to Wadebridge, to pay a visit to her cousins. She talks as if she should not be able to see you at Penryn; but I believe she will be mistaken.

I had lately with me, the person who has discovered the CHINA EARTH. He had with him several samples of the china ware, which I think were equal to the Asiatic. It was found on the back of VIRGINIA, where he was in quest of mines; and having read Du Halde, he discovered both the *Petunze* and *Kaolin*. It is this latter earth, which he says is essential to the success of the manufacture. He is gone for a Cargo of it; having bought, from the Indians, the whole country where it rises. They can import it for £13 per ton; and by that means afford their china as cheap as common stoneware; but they intend only to go about 30 per Cent. under the company. The man is a Quaker, by profession; but seems to be as thorough a Deist as I ever met with. He knows a good deal of mineral affairs, but not funditus.

I have at last hearkened to thy advice; and begin to commit to black and white, what I know in Chemistry, (I mean so far as I have not been obliged to other folks). Having finished my observations on furnaces, I intend to continue it as I have leisure; as it may be of use after my death.

Farewell dear Richard; and if I am to have an answer, let it be by next post, or it will not come to hand before my leaving home.

Thine affectionately, W. C.

B.—*Journey—Unlawfulness of Prize Dealing—* *Monthly Meeting, &c.*

To *R. Hingston.*

Honiton, 6th of 12th Mo. 1746.

Dear Richard,

As I am obliged to stay the night at this town; and have no business on my hands; I have sat down to employ the time in writing a few letters; which I suppose thou wilt take as a good sign, that my mind is freer than it has been for some time past; which indeed is the truth.   I having enjoyed, for the last 10 days, greater steadiness of spirits, than I had been favoured with for fourteen months before.   This I desire to be thankful for, as a peculiar favour; for I cannot find that my body is stronger, or in better order, than it was at my setting out on the journey.

I left Launceston the day after I wrote to thee from thence; and on my way to Exon, called on the widow Bidgood's family: and found my heart very near them.   There is certainly a good thing among them, though I fear there is too much of the stiffness of selfwill, in the old woman; the young ones are very tender, and would soon unite with friends, were it not for their mother; whom I pity, believing her to be an honest, zealous woman, but as I fear, mistaken.

I was out too late in the evening before I got to Exon, the cold pinching me sadly, so that I had flying rheumatic pains, and did not sleep half an hour, in the night preceding the meeting for business; and yet I was borne up to attend both that and the meeting of worship, in the afternoon.   We had nothing of business worth noting; only that the dealing in prize goods, is by an artful management, thrown back on our meeting. For though it was the unanimous sense of the quarterly meeting at Plymouth, that in case the meeting of sufferings did not give us a satisfactory answer, application should be made to the yearly meeting; yet by inserting the words *may be made,* which was doubtless purposely done; and by a poor quirk on them, the weight of the thing still rests on us. I have neither spirits nor disposition for debate, as I hope the affair will still go to London, in one shape or other; though I am sensible, the managing ones would be glad to stop it: but the work of Providence will be done; and as far as I am engaged in it, I hope not to neglect my duty.*

I was a whole week at Exon, not setting out till the frost broke up. At Bideford there hath been a considerable convincement, and there is room to hope there will be much more; so I was detained among them 4 or 5 days, much to my satisfaction, being wonderfully supported. Poor Jenny Scarven was among them some time before; and the service she had almost wore her out. But she is since bravely recovered; and the case was pretty much the same with me. I would fain, but cannot, enter into particulars; further than that I wrote Isaac Sharpells about the matter; and have since heard from good authority, that both he and Bay Kidd, who is in London, intend very soon to pay them a visit.

From hence, through troublesome roads, and very uncomfortable weather, I pursued my journey; and was at Spiceland monthly meeting, last 1st day was a week. Lawford (Godfrey) was there, and a good meeting we had; abundance of friends and others being at it. I got to Taunton last 3rd day week, and thought to have left it on the 6th or 7th day; but the weather partly stopped me over last 1st day. Mary Kirby being in company with Sarah Artis, and Mary Davis, at Bridgewater, had a concern not to attend that meeting, but to hasten on, and have an evening meeting at Taunton. She came in just as the afternoon meeting broke up. I was heartily glad to see her; and went to the evening meeting, which was large, and I hope attended with good service. Mary and I were the next day at J. Dymond's; a very honest friend, with a large family, about two miles from Town; attended by two young women, in whom I believe the truth is deeply and livingly at work. We had a sweet time among this family after dinner; and the waters being up, we had some difficulty to get back to Taunton; where we found Sarah Artis and the other friends, with whom we had a good meeting there the next day. Poor Taunton meeting begins to have some shinings of life in it, which I trust will increase. The women went on next morning for Minehead; and I came on to Ilminster, and to day here; Mary and Sarah Artis,

* It is now a rule of the Society, that members shall not deal in prize goods. *J. P.*

intended only to go as far as Exeter, but I believe they will go through the west. That Sarah Artis is a choice girl. Thus my very dear friend, I have given thee a short account of a long journey; I call it short, as I have not entered into particulars. Though the weather has been excessively bad, and I at times so low, that I have been ready to turn my horse's head homeward, yet on the whole, I have cause to be deeply thankful to the Almighty, Who hath pleased to let me experience, that He can carry through all difficulties; and so sanctifying them into the means of increasing our faith in His invisible power.

Adieu,

I am thy affectionate friend,

W. COOKWORTHY.

C.—*Sympathy.*

To *Richard Hingston*, Surgeon, Penryn, on the death of his second wife *Elizabeth Hingston*.

Plymouth, 24th of 4th Mo. 1747.

My dear Friends,

Whom I tenderly and truly love, and with whom I am made one both in suffering and in joy : I may say that my spirit has been deeply dipped in sympathy with you, for your great loss; and my heart is so bound up, that I hardly know what to say. But as I find and feel there is a sympathy between the members, so in the pure motion of it I am encouraged to desire and advise you, to look up for relief, to the head—to him who was touched with the feeling of our infirmities, who ever liveth to make intercession for us, and will not suffer us to be tried beyond measure; but as our eye is to him, he will support his poor depending children, and help them through all their afflictions. Of this my soul hath been, and is daily made a sure witness; for I have long dwelt in the house of mourning, and the Lord has blessed this habitation to me, as I hope he will do to you, my dear friends. For I clearly see that the Lord is at work in the earth, in a very signal manner; visiting the hearts of his creatures, in order to bring all into a nearer union with him; so that they may witness him to be their God, their alone strength and refuge, their all in all; and as we give up ourselves entirely to him, I question not but we shall witness, that all things will work together for good.

My poor dear Polly's case, turns out as J. Mudge thinks, and I believe, to be spinal: a melancholy case indeed, but though I can hardly look on the dear lamb without streaming eyes, yet hath the Lord enabled me to resign her to his will. Ah, can my soul say, he is worthy to be looked unto, for he is the only certain help, in the needful time.

I desire and advise, that Richard would not too much overdo himself. You can afford yourselves sufficient assistance, and are blamable in not making use of it.

I have called on your cousin Andrew, who is in the last stage of a consumption. I sat near two hours with him, and had so much satisfaction in my visit, that I have cause to hope the Lord is near him. Farewell my dear friends.

I am your sympathising friend,

WILLIAM COOKWORTHY.

D.—*Fatherly Tenderness and Religious Advice.*

To his daughter *Lydia.*

Plymouth, 12th of 12th Mo. 1749.

Dear Child,

I received thine by W. Frink some days since; and take it kindly thou wert so early in answering my last. The family being in usual health, the only news I have to send thee is, that this day week, thy Uncle Benjamin declared his intention of marrying with S. Collier; so that thou art like soon to have another Aunt. Whilst I sat in the meeting, my desires were very earnest, that thy Uncle might find the state into which he is about to enter, peaceable and happy; as through the favour of Heaven it proved to me and thy dear mother; and there is no question but all will find it so, who honestly endeavour to live in the fear of God, and behave to each other with that wisdom, love, and tenderness, which it leads to. Happiness, my dear, would not be a thing difficult to attain in any state of life, if people could but resolve to give themselves up to the direction of the Divine Being, and be governed by that truth, which he hath placed in every bosom; for want of which the world is like a wilderness, and full of confusion and trouble to the generality of mankind: the sense of which makes it my earnest desire, that I, and those who belong to me, may in a peculiar

manner, be separated from the love of the world and all its
follies, which I know to be vanity and vexation of spirit. I
have told thee above my regard for thy Uncle's welfare, and
how desirous I am that he may enjoy that happiness I and
your mother enjoyed. Think then what must be the tenderness and depth of my concern for you my offspring, the dear
pledges of that happy union; and almost the only remaining
visible comforts of my life, since it pleased Divine Wisdom to call
home your dear Mother, whose memory dwells as a sweet odour
on my spirit. That great Being, whose eye looks to the very
bottom of the heart, alone knows the frequency and strength
of those cries, which he begets in my soul for your everlasting
welfare.

It is for this alone I am concerned; being thoroughly satisfied, that if you are virtuous and religious, you will never want.
But my concern for your spiritual welfare, is truly great; and
mostly the subject of my morning sacrifice, when the God of
my life enables me to lift up you and your tender cause, as an
holy offering, before his altar. And as I have often entreated
the Almighty to keep your feet from the paths of vanity, and
preserve your tender spirits from the corruptions of the world;
so let me beseech thee, my dear child, to be strictly on thy
guard, against the love of anything here below. Learn to look
on every earthly object, as insufficient to give thee lasting
satisfaction or joy. No, my dear, nothing but endeavouring to
make thy thoughts and actions conformable with truth, can do
this; and it is the enjoyment of God alone, that can make thee
truly happy. Remember therefore thy Creator in the days of
thy youth, devote ever thy tender youth to his service, let thy
knees learn to bow before him, and offer the first fruits of an
innocent mind, in holy petitions for his care and watchfulness
over thee, and thanksgiving and praises to his great name for
his past mercies. Then wilt thou draw down on thy tender
spirit, the sweet influences of his Divine goodness; and engage his endless compassion, to make thee a blessing to thyself,
and a comfort to thy poor father. And let those truths be
engraven on thy heart; that provided meat, drink, and clothes,
are wholesome, warm, and decent, it is sufficient; and that to
endeavour to set thyself off, so as to gain honour from these
things, is an abomination in the sight of God; who only honours
those who honour him, by endeavouring, through his assistance, to adorn their spirits with humility, virtue, and piety.

I remain thy affectionate Father,

W. COOKWORTHY.

E.—*Affectionate Consolation.*

To *Ann Fox*, of Parr, in Cornwall on the death of her son, *Francis Fox*, at the age of 30, six years after his marriage to *W. C's.* daughter.

Plymouth, 28th of 2nd Mo. 1760.

Dear Sister,
Providence hath called on us once more for the exercise of resignation to the will of our Heavenly Father. This introduction will serve to let thee know that thou hast lost a worthy son. He was called home this evening, about 7 o'clock; after a week's sickness, in which he had nothing to do but struggle with the violence of his disorder.

What shall I say to thee? My poor heart is weak and worn out in deeply sympathising with his afflicted widow; whose grief for the loss of a most beloved Husband, to whom, as she now acknowledges, her heart was united from her childhood, is inexpressible. Never were a happier couple; nor ever was any relation more dearly beloved than my dear Francis was by us. It was impossible for me to have loved him with a more entire affection, had he been my own child; and I can with sincerity say, that I remember no action of his for which, in my inmost thought, I blamed him.

May the Comforter of his children, who look unto him to sweeten their bitter cups, by that arm which hath never failed to support them in the time of distress, give thee a fresh proof of his Almighty help; and enable us to say, The Lord gave and the Lord hath taken away, blessed be the name of the Lord.

I am thy true sympathising Brother,

W. C.

F.—*Travelling 80 years ago—Religious meetings— Swedenborg—&c.*

To his daughter—about 1777.

Wadebridge, 5th day, Evening.

Dear Lydia,
I am got thus far on my journey; which has hitherto, in regard to the service of it, been to my satisfaction; for which I hope I am duly thankful.

I passed a pleasant, peaceful evening at Cousin Browne's. They appear to me to be honest and worthy; and to fill up their place, in the order of Providence, with propriety; the children appear very promising, and I hope, from my feelings, that the blessing which makes truly rich is over that family. The old man appears to enjoy all the advantages which attend a useful well spent life: his old age is green, he is healthy and vigorous; his complexion may vie with that of youth, and there is something so placid and cheerful in his countenance, that I always looked on him with pleasure. But I forget that my paper is quarto.

Our friends at Germans were very kind. I had two very satisfactory meetings there; and as the meeting did not come on till 7, I found time to spend a few agreeable hours with the worthy Mistress of Port Elliott, and drank tea with her. She was extremely kind and I had no cause to repent of my visit.

As the afternoon was very rainy, I did not leave Germans till the evening. E. Eddy was in course my guide; but Cousin Stephen Fox was so politely kind, that he would too accompany me. We set out in pretty hard rain: as I had nothing but my surtout, he lent me his oil-case hood, which answered very well, so that I got through a severe rain without the least inconveniency; and he has lent me his hood through the journey. Our friend Rundle and his wife, received and treated me very kindly; and I had a tender, comfortable meeting with the few friends there, in the forenoon: his son-in-law, Allen, is a serious sensible young man; I bespoke him for my guide to Camelford, though he had never been there; but we got there in tolerable season, though too late for meeting. Indeed I was unequal to the service; as I was fatigued, and somewhat disordered by a very troublesome heartburn, of which I felt something the preceding days; but it hath quite left me and I am perfectly well.

We had a meeting at Camelford, next morning, with two friends who live in or near the town, and a few of the sober neighbours. We should have had a larger company, but the people were at harvest: tho' few, we were greatly favoured; and I believe several, if not most, said in their hearts. " It was good that we were here." Finding my mind quite cleared and easy, I and my young companion came on, and had an evening meeting at Port Isaac: It was well attended. Among others the Methodist preacher was at it. It was an open, satisfatory meeting, I believe I may safely say, to all that attended it. My Landlady behaved with her usual kindness and hospitality; and I was pleased with the widow Billing's company, who is a sensible and I believe a serious honest woman. She introduced me into the company of the Methodist preacher; few men have pleased me more: he is the exciseman there;—a very sensible man, of an unblemished character, and universally respected, as a man religious and of integrity: his principles are large and generous; and if he have any thing of the party spirit in him, I am persuaded it originated in a reverence for John Wesley. I spent a pleasing hour with him, in great openness of heart, and he bore us company as far as Endillion.

I came in here when the family were at dinner; and a large company they were, being swelled by the addition of G. Fox, sen. and jun. wives and two of their children; they received me cordially. After dinner, I went up to Cousin Edward's, who had expressed an impatience to see me. I want words to express the pleasure this worthy man's behaviour gave me. He looked cheerful and well; I expressed my pleasure at it, but at once his loving good heart was broke into such a sweet child-like tenderness, that melted mine along with it. I will not describe the scene;—it was such as thou wouldst naturally imagine it to be. I have the satisfaction of observing that his disorder has not in the least impaired his understanding; it is as good as ever,—nothing is hurt but his memory, so that at times he cannot hit on the names of things. He has lately had a fit of the gout, and is recovering; I write by his bedside; when I sat down to write he tenderly remembered to thee. Cousin Hannah is poorly, the rest of the family is well. It would have done thy heart good, to have heard the worthy husband speak of his wife; it was in the most simple language of love, from a heart that overflowed with it: theirs, I am fully satisfied, is the very conjugal union that Swedenborg speaks so much of: they are united in the eternal principle of pure love and are partners for ever. But how doth the great Father of all the families of the earth, own them as his children, in blessing them with a virtuous and worthy offspring. The son of peace is here, and notwithstanding the afflictions they have passed through, yet I doubt not but the promise, " Peace shall be in their dwellings" is fulfilled to them. Edward is this moment come in, so I must shut up for the present.

Farewell my dear children. May the good Lord ever preserve you in his pure fear; may you at all times, and for all things, look up to and depend on him, as a parent who is ever able, and ever willing, to protect and bless you; and, careful to keep here, you may safely leave the rest to his disposal. Remember me to your Sisters and to Manky: I hope my poor Brother is grown better, and that his family are well. My dear love is to them and to all my other relations and friends.

Farewell—Your affectionate Father, W. C.

G.—*Deep sympathy—His own privations—Friendship*
survives the grave.

To *Andrew Hingston.*

[No date.]

Probably written during the illness of A. H. who died in
1762.

I have thus far as thy sympathising friend
suggested every thing which occurs to me, which might be of
use in thy disorder; but the great medicine from above, the
sacred balm, the Almighty, the unerring hand of infinite
mercy, is the only certain cure, or alleviation of the sufferings
and ills, attending poor pilgrims, in their travel through this
vale of tears.   What a happiness it is to be in possession of
this knowledge! Long hast thou been in possession of it,
long hast thou looked to the God of Jacob as thy strength; and
he hath owned thee in thy own heart, by often lifting up the light
of His countenance upon thee, and being thy present help
in every needful time; and to those of thy acquaintance who
know and love Him, hast thou been truly near and honourable.   My heart embraces thee, whilst I write, in the love
which stretches beyond the narrow bounds of time, and is
immortal in its root, and claimeth kindred with every child
of the family of God.   Many such claims has my soul, in
particular, on eternity, or life would be an insipid way, a bitter
thing to me.   Genuine friendship is a plant from Heaven.
It bears the most precious fruit we taste below, but 'tis
eternity must exalt this fruit to its highest flavour.   Love,
the badge, the employment, the delight of the real Disciple
and true child of Christ, is and must be its own everlasting
reward.

I lost a father when very young; but he who hath been a
tender father to me, left me to honour his memory.   Dear
sisters of good dispositions, have been removed; a loving,
worthy and dearly beloved wife, the desire of my eyes, was
taken from me by a stroke.   My very dear friend, thy Brother,
was called home in the strength of life.   My tender mother,
dear to me by the natural tie, but inexpressibly so as a friend,
a spiritual helper, a sister in the best relations,—her too I have
lost, in the language of men.   But are all these dear souls
lost?   I trust not, for I cannot bear the thought: let me but
continue to labour to know him who is the resurrection and

the life, preserve and cultivate that life which he in infinite mercy has raised in me, and I have no doubt but I shall rejoin them, and never bo separated from them more; for well am I assured that true friendship survives the grave. Thou wilt judge, from what I have written, the state of my mind in regard to thee. Grave advice, to one who has endeavoured to live by supreme direction, would be nauseously impertinent; and consolation also, further than the overflowings of a friendly heart, ready to join him who sucks at the everlasting breasts. Calmly therefore, warm at heart, with brotherly love, with hopes full of immortality, for thee and myself, I dearly salute thee and thy spouse.

Remaining thy affectionate Friend.

W. C.

H.—*Disposal of China works.*

To *Ann Cookworthy*, Plymouth.

Bristol, 4th day, 10 o'clock.

My dear Cousin,

    When I wrote my last to thy father, I hoped to have left this city, last second day; but such hath been the nature of the affair which detains me here, that though I have endeavoured to the utmost of my power, to get it completed, I cannot yet succeed. The Attorney assures me that we shall have every thing ready by next 5th day; and if he is as good as his word, we shall finish our matters that evening, or the next day at farthest. And then if health permits, I shall set out in the machine, second day morning, and reach Plymouth on fourth day.

    I am heartily disposed to shew every mark of respect to a niece so sincerely and justly esteemed by me; and it hath been one source of anxiety and vexation to me, that I have so long been detained here; but there is really a necessity for my closing our affair before I leave this city. When this is done, I shall set my face towards Plymouth with great pleasure; not that I have any reason to complain of Bristol; for though I have had the load of important and difficult affairs on my mind, and have gone through a real fit of the gout in my side, I have been helped through all in the enjoyment of calm spirits, and inward satisfaction.

    I have a budget full of interesting matter for your entertainment at my return. I have not had the least reason to complain of R. Champion's behaviour; and all my acquaintance at Bristol, have shewn me much kindness and respect; and on the whole my time hath been spent agreeably amongst them, all things considered; for, considering my attention to China wares, the closing of my business with R. Champion, the settling the lovers' matters, which were in a much worse situation than we imagined: all this and the attending meetings, have made the last month the busiest one to me, that I have known for many years: but quiet dependance is sufficient to carry us safely and well, through all those things in which providence engages us. Let this be an encouragement to my dear niece through every difficulty she may meet with. Let us but determine in all things to do our duty, depending only on Him who is mighty to help; and nothing that can befall us can be hurtful to us. Let us learn to despise the superficial judgments of a world that looks only at the things that are seen, which renders all its specious wisdom foolishness in reality. Let the attainment and possession of a conscience void of offence regulate us in all our views and pursuits; and let us implore the help of the Great Father, and steadily wait for it, through the whole course of our conduct; and we shall know that blessing which maketh rich, and addeth no sorrow with it, to rest on our hearts and houses.

Farewell my dear cousin, and farewell all my dear friends. I am hastening to meeting. W. C.

I.—*Forgiving tenderness—Advice and consolation.*

To his daughter who had lately married imprudently without his consent.

Dear child,

As I have no doubt, but thy last letter to me contained the real sentiments of thy heart, I have several times read it with tenderness and satisfaction; for if thy wandering from the path of duty and peace, with the consequent trouble, distress, and remorse which I think thou must have undergone, have driven thee to the right place to meet with pardon support, and peace; and the goodness and tender mercies of a most bounteous Father have so shone forth, as to engage thy love and thankfulness, and have begotten a real thorough sense in the depth of thy heart, that he is the fairest of ten thousand, the only source of wisdom and bliss, the sure Almighty Protector and present help in every needful time; thou art in that place where I have often and ardently prayed

to see all my children.   I think I have naturally a heart not un-
feeling; thy outward prosperity, health and honour, would
give me some satisfaction, but all this, which the world is so
apt to doat on, appears trivial in my eyes.   We have no
abiding city here.   Eternity approaches us.   We know not
how near we are to an entrance on that immense ocean;
but a sense that those to whose existence I have been made
instrumental, are in the way which leads to everlasting happiness, would give me joy indeed.   Oh! that my dear children for
their own sakes, may give me my fill of this sacred comfort; I
have sometimes hoped, that they will endeavour to make grate-
ful returns for my parental love in this way, as they know that
nothing in their regard, could afford me so full a joy, as to
behold them God's children.

I say these things to strengthen thy good resolutions.   It
is not enough to run well for a season; we must set our hands
to the race in earnest, and expect to find many difficulties in it
which will call for constant care and strong exertion to sur-
mount.   We are all by nature children of wrath—the Devil
hath a deeper possession of our heart than we are aware of, and
he can only be cast out, as we are willing to part with our self love,
that inbred, worst enemy of our own house, without whose con-
current aid, the enemy of mankind would tempt us in vain.
How ready are we to see this self love in others!   How loth
to see and own it working in our own hearts.   Let us honestly stand open here to the silent though clear intimations of
heavenly wisdom, and be strictly on our guard against every
appearance of evil of this kind, and then the Almighty who be-
holdeth the proud afar off, but giveth grace to the humble, will
delight to bless us.   He will discover our enemy in all his
wily approaches, and in vain will the snare be laid, for the
child that is on its guard—delightful simplicity! offspring of
humility, resignation, and confidence in his help, who never
forsook his children, or sent them to the house of a stranger
to beg their bread.   How do I desire that I and mine may
possess more of thee; the heart fully possessed of thee is the
prodigal got home under the shelter of his father's roof, and
secure in his Almighty Protector.   That we live, move, and
have our being, in its Author; that he is the continual preserver
of that being he hath given us, the source of every blessing
of every kind which we enjoy; that man possesses nothing inde-
pendent of the Almighty, but his folly and corruptions, are
truths clearly demonstrable by the light of reason: but will
this demonstration give the heart that possession of them,

which may render it tranquil and happy? by no means: the world swarms with knowing philosophers who continue miserable for want of learning of him who was meek and lowly in heart; who, infinite in wisdom and power, is also plenteous in mercy and goodness; who waits, who longs, to give his creatures the knowledge of his salvation. The only terms are obedience to His laws, expressed by the easy yoke; and a willingness to serve and love him, by the light burden. My heart blesses, reverently blesses, the holy name of infinite love and mercy, who hath enabled me to set my seal to these truths, from the moment I was made willing to endeavour to live a life of order. I was never called to part with any pleasure or advantage which could add to my store of happiness, nor to the discharge of any duty but what actually added to it. I have often clearly seen the vanity of worldly wisdom and self dependence, by comparing the life of the worldly wise, to that of animals, the latter simple and perfect as they came out of the hands of their Creator, are fed and clothed by him; they simply do what his wisdom, in that way which is called instinct, engages and directs them to do; their necessities are thus provided for, and they are safe and happy in a degree suitable to their nature. But man is proud; man is artful, malicious, envious, and unkind; he refuses to submit to the laws of the family; sets up a separate footing of self interest, and self wisdom; sets his great Father at defiance; or, forgets that he hath such a Father: he is therefore unblest, and without repenting and returning, must be everlastingly so: for thus sowing to the wind, he must reap the whirlwind. Where christianity hath its due effect on our hearts, or as those vile affections are extirpated, we are brought to a practical acknowledgment of our Heavenly Father, by a life of continual dependence upon him. The mysteries of this life are learnt, in proportion to our humility and labouring after obedience to his will. I write, my dear, what comes into my mind—my paper is full; news, &c. I leave to thy sisters; and shall now take my leave; wishing you may try to live in that spirit the Apostle directs—Whatsoever things are true, whatsoever things are honest, whatsoever things are lovely, whatsoever things are of good report, if there be any virtue, if there be any praise, think of these things. With love to thy husband,

I remain thy affectionate father,

W. C.

K.—*Love of Christ, and Lightness of His Yoke.*

To *Esther Champion.*

Plymouth, 8th of 8th Mo. 1773.

I have hopes my dear Friend, that thy inclination to write to me was right, as since I received thy letter, my heart has been frequently deeply engaged on thy account. It gave me a tender joy to find that I had in any degree been instrumental to thy advantage, in the best regards; and I felicitate thee on thy being sensible of this advantage; as a heart turned in good earnest to God, as the source of all true peace and real happiness, should ever be numbered among his greatest blessings. Regard, therefore, this disposition of mind, as everlasting love to thee, and nourish it in thy heart, by the deepest thankfulness; and that this is a truth to which thou ought seriously and gratefully to attend, receive the evidence of his own words, " I have loved thee with an everlasting love, and therefore with loving-kindness have I drawn thee:" to be distinguished from the generality of mankind, who are lost amongst the vanities of the things of Time, by the eye turned towards the heavenly inheritance, as an honourable distinction! It is indeed, the foundation of all true honour, which all those will assuredly attain, who, weary and heavy laden, hear and follow the tender call, " Come unto me," and are diligent to learn of him who was meek and lowly in heart. I have a strong persuasion in my heart, that he hath allured thee into this school; and shewn thee, not only that these dispositions of soul are the way to peace, but, that they will render our conduct wise and beautiful. Let this therefore be the lesson of every day, yea, of every moment; looking steadily to the great giver of every good and perfect gift, for ability to govern every motion of thy heart by it; and thou wilt find that this humble sense of thy wants will draw down all needful supply; and in his meek spirit, wilt thou meet with his Almighty power, to give thee victory over all thy enemies, and make his yoke easy and his burden light. My heart overflows with gratitude, under the consideration of the lightness of his yoke; for what is it but being restrained from indulging our corruptions, and our follies? It is in reality, being eased of those weights and burdens, and that sin, which so easily besets us, which render the lives of poor mankind a miserable slavery; for knowing nothing of the glorious liberty of the children of God, whilst they are promising themselves liberty, they are the slaves of corruption: loaded and benumbed by this slavery, they are unfitted for every good word or work, and what is their reasonable service appears a heavy burden. But it is not thus with those who have attained, or are labouring after, the attainment of true peace and liberty. To do the will of their heavenly Father, they know, they feel to be their greatest happiness and highest honour. In their religious exercises or discharge of their other duties—"Oh what a weariness it is!" is never the language of their hearts. They feel that the employing their talents and abilities in fulfilling the will of the Great Giver, is the only worthy employment of them; and the testimony of a good conscience in regard to their motives, and the sense of help from above accompanying them, and the smiles of a merciful Father encouraging and rewarding their humble labours, render the burden of duty light.

The consideration of the infinite Almighty One, in calling such poor worms to be co-workers with him; the experience they have had of his goodness and tender mercies, and the clear perception, that it is his will that all should come to the knowledge of the truth and be saved, begets this cry in their hearts, "What shall I do for the Lord of Hosts?" Let us but endeavour to keep in this way, and every thing we meet with on our road will be blest to us; and made the means of our growth in wisdom, and in confidence in that arm, which will support and lead us in safety through all our trials, doubts, and difficulties, weakness, and poverty. Day unto day will utter speech, and night unto night shew wisdom; and "we shall know, if we follow on to know the Lord, his going forth to be prepared as the morning, and he shall come as the rain and as the latter rain on the earth." Mind not, therefore, any of these things which thou mayest suffer; but consider sufferings as honours, as lessons of wisdom, and as the permitted means of the Great General, to form such good soldiers as can endure hardships. Never endeavour to get rid of them by the diversions of company or amusement; but consider them as calls to duty and labour, which is the only lawful, beneficial way of getting rid of them; and when this is honestly done, thou wilt find thy mind opened and fitted for the enjoyment of all innocent recreations, social delights and satisfactions:— for though religion is careful, it is not a morose, formal, or severe spirit: "Little children love one another" is its invariable language. Innocence and simplicity make the safety, delight, and ornament of every child of the family, who are thus under the continual direction and blessing of that great Father, whose highest name is Love.

Remember me to the family, and be assured I am affectionately thy friend,

WILLIAM COOKWORTHY.

L.—*Doing well our law and help, and entire submission our wisdom.*

To *Philip Debell Tuckett*, on his marriage with *Esther Champion*.

Plymouth, 1773.

Dear Cousin,
    Thy letter of the 3rd current came to hand when I was at Germans, attending Francis Fox's funeral, and since my return, I have not, till now, found my mind in a proper disposition to answer it. I can say with great truth, that from the time of thy coming to Plymouth, I have had an affectionate regard for thee, and very warm desires for thy welfare. Thou hast always appeared to me as a young man of a good disposition, and a strong turn of mind towards virtue and religion; which hath encouraged me to hope, that thou wouldst become a worthy man, and a useful member of society. I have not the least thing in my heart, against thy connexion with E. C.; for whom I have a sincere and affectionate regard, as a young woman of great innocence, meekness, and sweetness of disposition; and if she continues a steady traveller, in the path in which Providence hath set her feet, I have not the least doubt but she will discharge, with propriety, the duties of the conjugal state, and in all the relations and concerns of it, prove a true help meet, and blessing to thee. This judgement is grounded on a presumption, that she hath been favoured with a sense of that blessing which maketh rich, and addeth no sorrow; which hath clearly satisfied her mind, that all things under the sun, as the means of contentment and felicity to an immortal spirit, without the gifts of his blessing, have vanity and vexation of spirit ever inscribed upon them. As this is my sincere judgement of thy Friend's character, I shall expect a spirit in her conduct, different, very different, from women in a common way ; and to her own peril be it, if she disappoints me. I will not allow her to order her economy and way of life. Custom is the law of fools.

She knows the Divine will is at once our law and help; and that our wisdom consists in putting the whole of our life under this direction; and our strength and success as we seek ability and support from him who is mighty, and able to save to the utmost. It is impossible for us to extend this principle too far; as our life will be wise and happy, just in proportion as we extend it. It dignifies every state that Infinite Wisdom may please to dispense to us; under its influence, the lowest state, by calling on us for the exercise of greater degrees of patience and resignation to the allotments of unerring wisdom, it raises us into actual elevation; whilst without it the Postchaise, the Coach, the fine furniture; and the gay fashionable life, have in truth no claim to a higher name than splendid baubles— It is a pitiable thing, that this truth is not enough attended to, by many religious people, who appear to content themselves with the discharge of what are called religious duties, as the whole of religion; and thus, while they appear to be strictly pious, order their lives, not by the wisdom of Christianity, but in the common style of the world. I give my pen a loose upon this subject; it is a very important one to you both.

It may possibly make some clear views, that may have offered themselves to my kind E. C. more clear; and tend to render some good resolutions she may have made, more strong;—in regard to thyself, I make no doubt thou takest it for granted, that the happiness of thy life is now settled on a sure basis; 'tis quite natural for young men in thy situation so to think, the illusion is pleasing; and thou mayest possibly complain of it, as an unkindness, to be awaked from this dream of happiness.—Happiness can only be the offspring of the fear of God; and that care, calmness, moderation, and diligence, which will ever attend it. To secure this happiness, thou must consider the state into which thou art about to enter, as requiring thy constant endeavour to behave with the utmost love, tenderness, and attention to thy partner; meekness and moderation are necessary to the discharge of these important duties; the most amiable disposition, the most assiduous love, and consummative prudence of a loving tender wife, never yet secured suitable returns from her partner; 'tis all indeed she can do: and in discharging her duty, she will receive the approbation of Heaven. If thou wouldst be a kind husband, watch against the spirit of the world as a man of business; for without great care, ability and success, with the honour which the world plentifully pours (in appearance at least) on the able and successful, are ideas that are too apt to

seduce from humility and simplicity of heart. Regard business as it stands in the Divine order; the means of exercising
honesty and beneficience, and the making a comfortable and
decent provision for thy family. Let all thy views tend to this
point, and look up steadily to Heaven for direction, and all
will be right; and the blessing of God will be found on all
that thou doest. Thou wilt then be a truly able tradesman,
and wilt be sure of meeting with the success that Providence
sees is the best for thee. Thou hast great cause to be thankful,
for the Providential care that hath hitherto been over thee;
the way to secure it in future, is to guard against elation of
mind and self-dependence; humility ever goes before honour,
and true humility is founded in Religion, and the knowledge
of God and of ourselves. Thou hast tasted of the good of religion; cultivate this experience, and rest assured that true
wisdom is attained by this cultivation. It is very likely I may
be at Bristol, early in the spring, by which time 'tis likely
your affairs may be closed. I sincerely wish you every happiness, and remain thy affectionate Kinsman,

WILLIAM COOKWORTHY.

M.—*Trust in God against difficulties.*

To *Esther Champion* on her marriage.

Plymouth, 6th of 2nd Mo. 1774.
My Dear Friend,
Before this will reach thy hands, thou wilt
have learnt that my family hath been in a distressed situation.
My daughter Hobson continues in a poor weak state; and my
daughter Fox, though bravely recovered, is not without her
trials. Her Franky is taken ill of the same disorder; but as
the seizure is moderate, and without alarming symptoms, we
hope he will do well. She behaves on this, and on every other
occasion, like one who hath been inured to affliction, and whom
experience hath taught where to apply, for support and ability
rightly to go through every trial and difficulty, that Providence
permits to be in her way.—I have been particular in giving
thee this account of my family concerns, as thou standest
numbered amongst the friends of my heart.

I cannot well close this letter, without giving thee a serious
word of encouragement, which I have a strong hope thou hast
a right to, and some persuasion thou mayest want :—my hope is,

Lightning Source UK Ltd.
Milton Keynes UK
UKHW020648070223
416609UK00011B/2444